Window Diaries

A COLLECTION OF POEMS

Alexis Jade

WINDOW DIARIES
Soft-cover edition 2024

ISBN: 979-8-9859153-3-4

For more information about special discounts for bulk purchases, please contact us at: **info@belluccipalmscarmichael.com**

Bellucci, Palms & Carmichael Publishing, LLC

DEDICATION

An ode to Italy in October.
The autumn that brought this all together.

ACKNOWLEDGMENTS

I'd like to thank my family who through everything we have separately been through, we have made it this far together.

Thank you to my dear friends who have given my heart hope in a connection I never thought I'd feel. You have inspired me.

To my publisher and editor, thank you for seeing in my words what I have always hoped to share. The opportunity has encouraged me to be the poet I want to continue to be.

To my sister; my strength, my light in the dark, my reminder of the best days ahead, thank you for being you. You are forever my favorite thing about living.

And to the One who has so lovingly kept me throughout it all, my soul says thank you.

I love you all.

CONTENTS

Heaven on Earth

From the stars I was born.
Like water, I flow.
Like trees, I grow.
On Earth I was formed.
Thank you.
Now all in love I will adorn.

Compass

An infinite amount of chances, options, and paths.
Through change and redirection, our souls navigated
here.
Almost to return back.
Like this was where we were always meant to be.

When It's Just Us Pt. 1

When it's just us the curiosity of my heart calls me
closer.
The sweet ring of your voice; I pick up every time.
We speak and your words flow through me.
Like being able to feel music.
Feeling as if it were a tangible object.
Like the notes themselves are dancing in the palms of
my hands.
A kind of balletic movement that carries me off these
feet into a place beyond just here.
A place I float.
A place only we know.

Ships In The Night

You can harbor them in.
You can dock and observe.
Maybe take sail and begin to fly.

But when night falls, the seas change.
Some souls like the passing waves, merely appear to
show and continue.
To grow you and go.
A lasting presence only in the love they imparted.

Stained Glass

Since you
my heart shattered in a new way.
A poetic kind of broken.
Pieces creating a vibrant mosaic of the place in which
I'd always kept so hidden.

Two Souls Don't Just Meet

By no accident is it that these souls
although estranged
have come together to form a crash
that shatters the shallow perceptions of those whose
hearts
have yet to feel the allure
of a not so accidental collision.

Soon

Be patient, young lover.
Listen, old soul.
Someday it will all come together.
The pieces will fall into place.
The moments will all tie as one
and suddenly you'll realize your life had already begun.

Why

I often wonder why I ever wondered about you at all...

Incurable

The ache of vulnerability afflicts my heart.
As if every moment of openness stabs the very nerve I
am trying to heal.
Severed,
with no hope of mending.
Antidote?
Speech.
But for the labor of this remedy there is no
compensation.
Only the raw veins of an exposed wound.

Bad Meal

I can't help but wonder why we blend?
Where what is similar is not familiar,
so searching elsewhere for a difference is the answer.
Maybe the never arriving satisfaction caused by the
sameness forced us to blend
because of the fear of the same distaste left on plates
before.

Dreamer

Closed eyed, anything is possible.
So put me to sleep, let my eyes go closed for longer.
Because in the dark, there are dreams.
In the night
there is a magic I never want to leave.

When It's Just Us Pt. 2

Us feels like sitting on the shore seated at the edge
where the water kisses the land over and over again.
A kiss from the tender lips of the ocean that are forever
promised to the soft sand.
Each day without reservations, they meet with passion.
A beautiful cycle of a love so infinite;
I, the soft sand and you, the tender sea.

Scared

How quickly fear engulfs.
With a change, a thought…
it enters.
Unraveling all you know to be the ultimate truth of your
Being which is;
You are love and where love lives fear cannot inhabit.
But all at once, it's diminished.
The Knowing.
Like you never knew at all…

Il Finale

Without you I felt no music.
The melody of my heart was muted.
The violin strings had seen their last strokes.
Curtain.
But now on this silent stage,
I wonder if the quiet was what I needed all along.
That maybe you were just noise.
No song at all.
Merely a divergent forte.

Franco Zeffirelli Museum After Lunch

So much wine.
It's fine.
I didn't decline.
Aged well.
Too swell.
Let's dwell.
But the good kind.
With a soft mind.
There I think we can find
a love beyond space and time
that no one could ever define.

5... 6... 7... 8

His laughter is what I noticed first.
A sound so melodic, like a perfect allegro.
A giggle to a crescendo.
An enticing piece that vibrates every part of my heart.
And since, there has been no greater song.

SOS

When did love become something so hard to grasp?
Like gasping for air in a turbulent bitter sea,
love to me has become a strain.
A chore that is never complete.
Like dishes in the sink piling after days of poorly
prepared food that never quite satisfied the hunger of a
starving heart.
The hunger that cries for the satiation that comes with a
warm hug or the safety of a soft kiss.

Further Away

I want to feel close
but sometimes the closeness feels like the conjunction
of two planets.
All at once they move through the sky
and from my vantage point on Earth,
they seem to be keeping perfect time.
Lined up as if to be engulfed in each other.
But again, my eyes deceive.
No two planets are ever that close.
Millions of light years separate each one.
Yet to me, they lovingly touch.

Apartment In Naples

As I sit on my balcony
the sounds of the town are below
I look down to see if they know
Do they know I ponder?
That I think and I wonder?
They hustle and speed
They move so quick
So fast
So swift
They sadly miss
The drift of the wind
The smell of the sea air
They must not seem to care
But what do I know
I'm merely above
pondering, thinking, and wondering.

A Lesson From My Dream

Give yourself the gift of time
Though just an idea
Made up
The essence of time is real
There are transformations in the passing of her.
Whatever you may call the moments that happen and
disappear, "time" is a healing concept.
Where the linear and nonlinear occurrences of her
create new hopes

Time creates all that is good.
Keep her.
Honor her.
She is your ally here.

A place governed so closely by her
but not as a tyrant leader but a gentle teacher.
Allow time to show you the truth, the beauty, the love.
Trust her.
She's the healer, revealer, life giver.

Urgent Reminder

Don't rush.
Be still.
Keep it simple.
Nothing is more urgent than peace.

Respond

I hate that I'm the girl that always picks up.
Links up.
Always has time to pull up.
Sweep up.
I sweep up all your mess.
Which I guess is much less tragic than forever giving
you my best.
The best and all the rest.
Here's the rest of what I have because by now you have
drained every tear and hung up all my fears.
Hung out to dry.
I don't know why.
I hate that I'm the option.
The maybe.
The one day.
The possibility.
When will I be picked up?
Linked up?
Pulled up?
Swept up?
I'd love to be the girl that was more.
The one that was the best.
Better than the rest.
Tears and fears dissolved
Because I went from an option to the final answer.

Please

Forgive.
Be Freed.

Walking In The Rain In Tuscany

A journey into the night so cold, where every step chills
my bones.
They rattle beneath my skin, shaking enough to pierce
my fragile flesh.
Revealing to me the depths of my soul.
Those parts that desire to feel a love grander than any
love before.
Grander than the rains that pour out of the sky for miles
ahead.
Warmer than the sun that for now hides in the clouds.
But soon, like the sun, my love will shine through.
I'll finally come to know what it's like to not be
walking alone.

Flooded

Stimulate me with speech.
Conversation please come.
Brainstorm.
Already so wet with wisdom.
Water me more with your words.
A climax like a complete sentence.

My Favorite Day

I think about you when leaves fall,
when I feel small,
and sometimes not at all.
I like those moments the most.
The moments where my mind is free from wanting you,
hoping for you,
and tirelessly longing for you to remember the time
when I was the one you were falling for.

Creators

Choice of word is one of our biggest phenomenon.
The ability to reconstruct even the most complex
scenarios with just a few simple words.
Or the power to tear it all apart.
The more I think about it
I see how much power we hold.
With these words we take for granted, use so loosely
and vague,
we carry this capacity to create anything.
Make nothing into something
or have everything come to an end.
Or begin for that matter.

How

I forgive you for always hurting me.
But I don't know how to forgive myself for
continuously letting you.

Distance

I see you for who you are.
Even when you get lost in the fog.
I see you.
I accept you for who you truly are.
Because who you are is more than all of this.
The fog.
The walls.
The blinders.
The falls.
Who you are is much more.
It's so much that I can see no one but you.
Just you.
With you is where I want to be.
I want to see you for longer than the stretch from here
to the moon
Or the space between where I lay and you stay.

Hiding

I pray one day you stop hiding from the love that so passionately seeks you.

The Recital

I feel like I've journeyed to this place where the
observer and experiencer meet.
Seeing life and feeling it all at the same time.
A story of duality like no other.
Able to bear witness and actually feel too.
Where the audience and performer become one.
And there goes the dance of life.

The Discovery

You don't even know me…
What is knowing me?
Or knowing anyone or anything…
How can you?
Everything is a mystery.
You don't even know me, yet, you knew me to be one
you'd like to know.
You know you love me, want to kiss me, hold me,
touch me.
All this knowing what you want like you have always
known me.

And it is only now that, to be known by you is no
mystery.
Because you've come to know me through love.
The most known thing of all.

Lost In Tuscany

I got turned around, to be found again.

Lost At Sea

Sometimes when I rise I don't hear the birds.
Sometimes behind the blinds there are no sounds to be
found.
Only the sulk of my heart that lies searching.
Charting towards some chime where parts of this heart
that breaks can find fuel to sail out of the darkness that
so silently deafens me.

Slipping

I made this vortex.
One that travels deeper with every "yes" when I meant
"no"
My precious truths swallowed up with only one to
blame,
myself.
Why have I allowed this destruction?
They hear my "of course" and it sounds like I care,
but I don't.
I care to love, but I hate.
I hate to disappoint, yet each night I'm reminded of
how often I disappoint myself.
When did this happen?
This vortex of boundless upheaval that unravels the
purity of my once honest heart.

On Our Way Somewhere Forever

If I ever say I want to go somewhere, interject.
Say somewhere you'd rather go.
Let's look at both.
I want to know your opposite places.
We can discuss, compromise, compare.
Let's discover together.
Nothing is definitive.
All can be changed, different, and new.
Where a meeting of the minds can lead to an adventure
of a lifetime.

Wrong Questions

It's always, what are you doing to get closer to your destination?
Never, what are you enjoying about the journey?

What Is Love?

I say love all day but do I have any idea what it is?
I love my cat.
But I also love food.
I love Earth.
And also love you.
They say there's different kinds of love.
Okay?
Which one is for me?
Can they all be felt at once?
Are they categorized by situation, place, or thing?
But I thought love was universal?
Meant to be unconditional?
A kind of communal love that's all encompassing.
Full of graciously accepted understandings.
How do you compartmentalize when the definition calls
for complete openness?
What is love?
What is love?
What is love?

Time

Simultaneously bringing us together and further apart.
An imagined concept that rules the sequences of our lives.
Healing hearts that are broken, while shattering the souls of others.
A ticking reminding us that she indeed is passing.
But that same sound plays like a melody that moves you.
And with acceptance of her song,
She fills you with hope.

Dialogue

I spent time with myself.
Just I alone.
Simply amongst the trees and wind and sun.
All at once I was swayed to chill in the rays.
As I laid, I told myself to listen.
Between the request and the next breath, I listened...
Silence.
And alas the message was heard.

Illusion

Even in obstacles, there is no obstacle at all.
Only the belief that there is and believing is merely a
choice.
Knowing now you can choose a different belief, makes
obstacles an illusion of thought.

Reminder

We can do less and get more.

Desire

The problem with desire? ...
It's that we forget it's all we have.
The very thing that animates the millions of cells in our
being
seems to be this word desire.
Breathing, eating, sleeping; our bodies desire to
function.
Meditation, walks, books; my soul's desire to
illuminate.
Desire is the overtaking force that turns a thought into a
city or a wish into true love.
The encouraging fuel that makes all possible.
Your highest self, your reason for existence,
In your deepest desires you will find.

Breathe

The end isn't as close as it feels.
The beginning isn't as far as it seems.
Or vice versa.
The limitation of distance between the now you
experience and where you would ultimately like to be
is only as far apart as the next breath.

Canvas

We're all a canvas being painted each day of our
existence,
later to be revealed
the masterpiece that is us.

Redefined

Melancholy is art, not a state of mind.

Spectator

Hand me the clearest spectacles,
but only to spectate
never to be skeptical,
because I'm here.
And where I am is where I'm meant to be.
Here to spectate and see.

Perfect

Perfection is more than we think it to be.
Perfection does exist.
It's a universal concept that simply means all is
happening just as it was intended.
Always.

The Beauty Of Life

This is happening.

Rest in it.

Made in the USA
Columbia, SC
13 July 2024

38573778R00036